FINDING OTHERS TO LOVE

Healing Self Esteem, Building Resilence

Lily Leroy

TABLE OF CONTENTS

CHAPTER 1: LETTING GO

Relationships with narcissists every now and again end regardless of how hard you attempt to spare them. The end is regularly agonizing, debilitating, and by and large upsetting. Regardless of whether your relationship closes, drapes together for quite a long time or years, or sinks into a musicality that you can live with, you should figure out how to relinquish a significant number of the desires, expectations, and dreams you have had about how you needed it to function. Changing your viewpoint, assumptions, responses, and procedures will decrease your disappointment, enthusiastic wounds, and general misery.

1. CHANGE YOUR PERSPECTIVE

At this point you comprehend that the narcissist's perspectives on the world, connections, and of you are contorted, and his responses aren't typical. The most widely recognized explanation you consistently get bushwhacked by the narcissist's responses is that you continue believing that he'll respond typically. It's particularly hard to remember this when the narcissist is by all accounts talking and interfacing all the more routinely for a while. You find a workable pace he has returned to focus and will currently be sensible. Be that as it may, the narcissist's turned perspectives will consistently re-emerge, so you should be readied.

- Narcissists Will Always Be Narcissistic
- Overcome Your Fear of Being Judgmental
- Quit Superintending

2. CHANGE YOUR REACTIONS

- Let Go of Winning and Losing

- Only You Have the Right to Judge Yourself
- Stop Hiding—Tell Others What You're Going Through
- Be Yourself Instead of What Others Want You to Be

3. CHANGE YOUR STRATEGIES

- Stop Showing Your Reactions to the Narcissist
- Restrict Your Contact with the Narcissist
- Set Real Boundaries and Limits
- Step Away from Conflict
- Protect Yourself

4. CHANGE YOUR LIFE

- Tune In to Yourself
- Reflect on How You Were Vulnerable to the Narcissist
- Reassess Your Friends
- Don't Get Stuck in the Past
- Future Fears
- Reach Out to New Opportunities.

CHAPTER 2: HOW TO GET OVER THE NARCISSIST HURT

Despair

Torment, outrage, and melancholy are altogether bound up together. Outrage keeps the agony of despondency and misfortune under control until we are sufficiently able to hold up under it. Distress communicates our most profound agony so it can turn out and be mended. Elizabeth Kubler-Ross says that we experience five phases of despondency when we experience an incredible misfortune: disavowal, outrage, dealing, gloom, and acknowledgment. In fact we hover through these emotions all around as we mend and gradually deal with reality that our lives are changed until the end of time. Owning and communicating your anguish permits you to know when you are harming, furious, and wilfully ignorant. There is a lot of you can do to recuperate these sentiments as they rise. It's additionally useful to know about when you are haggling with yourself and attempting to return to how things were, which drives you once again into the agony. As you lose trust, it tends to be acceptable to realize that you're feeling of melancholy is really an opening to the plausibility of acknowledgment.

In our quick, pick up the pace and-get-over-it culture, there is a supposition that anguish should last two or three months and be finished. Be that as it may, it is critical to remember that you're grieving numerous misfortunes when your relationship closes with a narcissist. You've lost a companion/sweetheart/accomplice. You've lost the fantasy of what you accepted your life would resemble with that individual. Your confidence has been harmed because of the accusing and cheapening by the narcissist. You've likely lost property, cash, and money related soundness. Your certainty and feeling of worth have been destroyed. You may have lost portion of the time you used to go through with your kids. You've lost your relationship objectives. What's more, what's more, the narcissist is most likely despite everything staying nearby taking steps to make your life hopeless.

Managing Denial

At the point when you've been a guardian for such a long time, it's frequently difficult to admit to yourself as well as other people the full degree of the damage you've endured in your relationship with the narcissist. You're progressively happy with focusing on the narcissist's agony or the exertion and guarantees he is making. You need to continue trusting that if the narcissist just finds support, things will pivot. Investigating your own torment, checking up all that you have lost, and truly conceding that you have been surrendered can appear to be humiliating and excessively difficult. Your inclination to assume all the fault for the disappointment of the relationship onto yourself may make it harder for you to recognize the profound wounds you have continued.

Recognize the Harm That Was Done

You're not to fault for the manner in which the narcissist treated you. Narcissists make a solid effort to keep you wobbly and helpless. Your altruism, liberality, and adaptability were exploited. Have a go at taking a gander at the mischief that you encountered without making a decision about yourself. It might be hard for you to quit assuming liability for how the narcissist treated you, however it's indispensably significant that you separate his conduct from yours. You didn't make the narcissist treat you seriously. The narcissist decided to treat you that approach to abstain from feeling awful himself.

Experience the Feelings

At the point when you recognize the mischief you encountered, it raises undesirable and in some cases overpowering sentiments. While you were in the relationship with the narcissist, you believed you expected to maintain a strategic distance from these emotions so as to continue onward. Rather, you consistently centred on the narcissist's emotions and attempted to keep things positive, perky, and pleasant for him—and for yourself. During the time that those upsetting encounters were going on, it's feasible you made a decent attempt to disregard how harmed you were. That refusal of your emotions kept you in the relationship, maybe longer than was beneficial for you. It additionally kept you from truly observing, feeling, and monitoring the truth of your injurious circumstance.

Outrage Is Normal

Obviously you're furious. Partners are more ready to feel hurt and bitterness than they are outrage. Outrage is critical in the mending procedure. It's a characteristic reaction to being hurt, to having your limits stomped on, and to being controlled and utilized by others for their own motivations. Your needs, needs, inclinations, emotions, sentiments, and decisions were overlooked and negated by the narcissist, while he limited and trampled your character and confidence. You ought to be irate.

Outrage Is Motivating

Outrage is an invigorating feeling. It pushes you to activity. It propels you to ensure yourself and engages you to move yourself away from hurt. Outrage is not something to be embarrassed about. In your relationship with the narcissist, you were presented to his lost and manipulative resentment. That isn't the sort of outrage I'm discussing here. You should be in contact with your upright indignation.

Narcissists deliberately attempt to combine you into an impression of themselves. You should think the same, feel the same, and carry on the same. Your feeling of self, your entire character, was deliberately being dispensed with. Outrage is the suitable and important reaction right now. It's there to protect your singularity, character, and confidence. By denying your displeasure right now, left your self-esteem open to harm. Right now is an ideal opportunity to bring back indignation into the image to push you toward caring more for yourself.

Haggling, Delaying, Buying Time

At the point when you become mindful of how you have been abused and exploited, carrying your outrage and hurt to the surface, it's anything but difficult to need to push these contemplations and sentiments away and simply return to how things were. All things considered, there were additionally numerous beneficial things about your relationship; it surely wasn't all terrible. Truth be told, you may in any case feel some affection and thinking about the narcissist. Those sentiments don't simply dissipate immediately. There is a lot of that you miss on the grounds that there were likewise charming, possibly brilliant, times. You might be feeling regretful that maybe you didn't do everything you could to make the relationship work. This is haggling.

It's difficult to retain this colossal change in your life at the same time. You need time to assess, comprehend, think back to see things from another point of view. Narcissists energize self-question. Your psyche gets loaded with "possibly . . . what if . . . assuming as it were." Bargaining is the manner in which we purchase time to thoroughly consider things and to test whether there is any alternative conceivable other than all out relationship breakdown.

This haggling time likewise permits you to pick up quality, learn new aptitudes, thoroughly consider your choices, hear others' thoughts, construct support, and all in all set yourself up to face this new reality. It is entirely expected to course through the sentiments of disavowal, outrage, and haggling again and again as you get acclimated with your new life circumstance. Progressively the pieces set up themselves. As you think about the narcissist's practices from these new points of view, your bearing turns out to be progressively clear.

Discouragement

Despair is profoundly awkward and makes it hard for you to need to take part in the great occasions that others appear to have.

Misery is difficult to do alone but then awkward to feel or communicate in typical social settings. You feel like a killjoy. Furthermore, you're correct; numerous individuals do abstain from being around other people who are discouraged. Likewise, you can't constrain yourself to get past your sorrow snappier. In this manner, quite a bit of your lamenting methods being separated from everyone else and regularly ruminating, filtering through recollections, working through your hurt and outrage, and presumably an excessive amount of self-analysis. The entirety of this can be profoundly difficult.

Sadness

Melancholy is the thing that some have called "the dim night of the soul. "Hopelessly, you feel that you have lost everything, and you have no clue how you're going to adapt to all the progressions and choices you're confronting. You trust you don't have the foggiest idea how to go ahead, don't have the solidarity to proceed, and have no bearing. You may feel sad and vulnerable. You might be enticed to fury and tempest or breakdown and surrender.

Hopelessness is an amazingly upsetting encounter. However it is something everybody has or will experience. It can likewise be a profoundly illuminating time of revelation. At the point when we feel at our least, we face the unavoidable chance to get past it in any case. It's the premise of the proverb for Alcoholics Anonymous— "each day in turn." You get past this minute, this hour, this day, this week, this month. Every day you find new qualities, points of view, and potential outcomes. What's more, a large portion of us detest each moment of it.

Incredibly, despair is a mending experience. It cements that the past is softening endlessly. It requests that you take a stab at something new—another idea, another mindfulness, another answer. It drives you into conclusive acknowledgment and introduces the arrangements you need.

Connect—Get Support

Lamenting can be amazingly forlorn, and the majority of your loved ones become worn out and prepared to proceed onward a long time before you have arrived at the finish of your sorrow. On the off chance that you haven't done as such previously, right now is an ideal opportunity to connect for master and concentrated help—an advisor, a separation recuperation gathering, or a profound counsellor. In spite of the fact that it tends to be hard to request help, help yourself that getting out to remember a narcissistic relationship is a more than normal awful experience. It's difficult for anybody to traverse it without the additional support, help, and genuine comprehension from individuals who are prepared to perceive and treat the perplexing enthusiastic inability of narcissism.

This is additionally a decent time to take a gander at the aptitudes and apparatuses you may need to defeat your inclination to be a partner. What keeps you so hyperaware of someone else's agony thus unmindful and inert to your own? For what reason would you say you will endure but you can't stand it when others feel even the littlest dissatisfaction? Do you have just a couple or a large number superintending practices? This is a decent time to figure out how to more readily adjust your needs with those of the ones you love.

Show restraint

Recollect that lamenting requires some serious energy. The time it takes you to get past this can't be contrasted with anybody else's. Be benevolent to yourself right now. Treat yourself affectionately and with sympathy. Set aside your self-reactions and consider how you would treat a dear companion experiencing this equivalent sort of misfortune. What might you say to her or him? Direct those sentiments toward yourself again and again until you genuinely feel sustained and thought about.

Tolerating What Is

Acknowledgment happens when you see plainly that there truly is no returning to what was. Regardless of what you or the narcissist do from here on, things won't be the equivalent. Acknowledgment can carry with it a sentiment of sadness from the outset since you're at long last and completely feeling your misfortune. Be that as it may, acknowledgment gives you the understanding to push ahead and make better outcomes. It likewise brings a feeling of opportunity and alleviation when you aren't stuck in those ineffective persecutor/injured individual/rescuer practices with the narcissist any more. You can be progressively transparent about what you think, feel, and need to do. You presently realize that you are never again answerable for anything the narcissist does. You presently have choices that weren't there previously.

Try not to Build Your Life around Grief

Confronting reality with regards to this relationship can discharge your vitality and consideration regarding use individually life and feeling of self-esteem. Be that as it may, you can get soiled down in at least one of these melancholy and misfortune affections for quite a long time or years in the event that you don't stay mindful of your objective—making another and better life for yourself.

Try not to Get Stuck

A lot of outrage can transform into disdain, harshness, or retribution. Or then again you may get secured in haggling— particularly on the off chance that you fear change, keep on accepting you're liable for the narcissist's sentiments and activities, or anticipate that yourself should keep keeping guarantees that the narcissist has broken or dismissed. In the event that you can't take advantage of your internal quality, skill, and self-esteem, you may fall into overpower and rout. Keep mindful of which emotions you are attempting to mend, and notice whether you are stalling out in any of them. Get backing and help on the off chance that you don't appear to be pushing ahead.

Constraint

Imagining that all is well, denying that you need assistance or backing, denouncing your weakness, or not permitting yourself to really grieve your passionate wounds would all be able to postpone the recuperating of your misery and torment. They can putrefy and blast out of resentment, dread, uneasiness, or long haul sadness. At that point when another misfortune tags along in your life, the uncertain anguish of this misfortune can build your enthusiastic response to that occasion. Working through your pain currently can invigorate you the, stamina, and certainty to deal with other troublesome circumstances later on.

Overpowering Shame and Guilt

Putting down yourself, condemning and demonizing your responses, and judging and criticizing yourself as you lament will make sentiments of disgrace and blame. Disgrace is particularly weakening and confines your mending procedure since it basically characterizes your feeling of self as terrible, useless, and undeserving. The narcissist utilized fault and allegation to move his own sentiments of disgrace onto you. Try not to take on this projection from the narcissist. You are not blameworthy of making the narcissist state, feel, or do—anything.

Find New Meaning for Your Experiences

New Understanding

The cutting off of any relationship can achieve new getting yourself and the other individual. The loss of your affection, expectations, and dreams has been fantastically baffling and demoralizing. Having the option to see and comprehend the realities of what was happening in the relationship can be a consolation. At the point when you see these examples, you have a superior possibility of recognizing and maintaining a strategic distance from this sort of relationship later on. As you recoup, you'll find that the misery work you have done encourages you feel more grounded, rational, and strong.

See Your Inner Strength

As your despondency settle, you'll see that you have another attention to your inward quality. You confronted circumstances you never figured you could. You learned new abilities and reactions that have given you a more noteworthy feeling of certainty. You're increasingly keen and shrewd. You're less regularly astounded and increasingly arranged to deal with troubles that emerge. You're more on top of your qualities, inclinations, sentiments, emotions, and rights. These might be qualities that you didn't have any acquaintance with you had before this misfortune.

Expanded Humbleness

You've additionally discovered that you can be profoundly harmed, you can't recuperate the narcissist, and you can't do everything all alone. You're flawed, you're not strong, and you need assistance from others. You're powerless, but then the earth didn't deteriorate. You discovered you could really deal with more than you suspected. You presently realize solidly what number of individuals love you. Your life is progressing forward and—shockingly—in any event, showing signs of improvement. Recollect that an emergency incorporates peril—and this has genuinely been a hazardous entry. It likewise incorporates opportunity. As you rise up out of your sorrow, you'll rethink your capacities.

Knowing your frailties and restrictions and going past them manufactures certainty. As you tackle each difficult issue in turn, you gain gratefulness for the way that life is troublesome however can be overseen. You've gotten prepared, experienced, less gullible, all the more perceiving, and caring toward yourself and the battles of others.

CHAPTER 3: HEALING SELF ESTEEM

Your contemplations and decisions about yourself and your circumstance, alongside the assets you have accessible, are in reality more significant than the occasion itself. This section tells you the best way to fix the manner in which you take a gander at yourself and your circumstance, re-establish your trust in yourself, and recapture prosperity, quality, and inspiration.

Mending Your Damaged Self

You Are Not the Cause

You thought the narcissist was going to make your life great, and now you have discovered it was the exact inverse. You can most likely despite everything recall the great occasions, when you felt everything going perfectly and you were the sole focal point of the narcissist's consideration. That was a strong inclination—even addictive. Be that as it may, the narcissist has different sides, and now you are confronting the opposite side. You generally get both.

You didn't make the narcissist admire you, nor did you cause the narcissist's present threatening vibe, fault, and dismissal. Those practices are altogether heavily influenced by the narcissist, not you. Stop, at this moment, assuming any liability for the narcissist's activities. Start focusing on your own practices and spotlight on settling on decisions about what you need and need to improve. Making a move causes you move out of the sentiment of being an unfortunate casualty.

You Don't Have to Be a Victim

Despite the fact that you have been deceived by the narcissist, you don't need to feel or act like an injured individual. In the event that you change the mark of unfortunate casualty to the word disillusioned, it's stunning how much this progressions how you consider your present circumstance. At the point when you distinguish yourself as an unfortunate casualty, you wind up feeling miserable and powerless. You will in general spotlight on just your agony, limiting your qualities and neglecting the individuals who love and care about you. You want to surrender. You feel singled out and some way or another a disappointment.

At the point when you distinguish your emotions as dissatisfaction, it encourages you characterize your circumstance such that you realize you can deal with. All things considered, who hasn't been disillusioned? You've adapted to dissatisfactions previously and gotten over them. This might be an a lot greater frustration, however, you are simply making changes that you don't care for and that don't fit with what you thought would occur. That is disillusionment. Here are a few models:

It is difficult to revamp your life when you consider yourself to be a disappointment. It leaves you with no expectation. Then again, considering this to be as a failure, rouses you to think about the master plan of your life. You can consider yourself to be all in all, and your encounters are only a piece of that entirety. It's simpler when you recall that there are others who love you, care about you, and bolster you. You have aptitudes, attributes, and capacities that you can use to re-establish your life. Considering this to be as an undesirable change, as opposed to as a catastrophe, can prod your imagination and critical thinking capacities to bounce in and begin reacting.

Give Yourself Compassion

You're not an awful individual, nor are you moronic or wrong since this relationship has finished. Almost 50 percent of all relationships in the United States end in separate. Clearly you wouldn't mark all of those individuals as contrarily as you're naming yourself.

You'll improve your confidence tremendously by being increasingly sympathetic toward yourself. Chat with yourself the manner in which you would to your dearest companion in the event that she or he were experiencing this equivalent experience. What might you say to facilitate the torment? What uplifting statements would you give? You wouldn't be compromising, denouncing, accusing, or pretentious. Stop every one of these types of self-judgment. Negative self-assaults are extra rehashes of what the narcissist has said to you. Relinquishing the narcissist incorporates relinquishing his negations and intentionally deciding to treat yourself in an all the more adoring and chivalrous way.

Relieve Your Body

Basic your misery are body sensations and crude feelings that really cause torment, weakness, low vitality, and lack of care. At the point when you experience a twisting encounter, your body can get pain-filled, tense, and jittery, making it hard to eat, rest soothingly, or recuperate from feeling constantly depleted. In the event that you don't deal with your body's reactions to every one of these burdens, it can get powerless against headaches, intestinal bombshells, spinal pains, and significantly increasingly genuine illnesses, for example, immune system reactions and melancholy.

Try not to ignore great physical consideration. Distinguish your top pick, solid nourishments and ensure you generally have them close by. In case you're feeling irate, hard, crunchy nourishments can assist you with feeling much improved. In the event that you are harming or feeling low, delicate, smooth nourishments can be encouraging. Deliberately consider the nourishments you are eating and pick ones that cause you to feel great. Linda lived on shrimp for a month after her separation. Henry bit through two pounds of carrots and said it sincerely mitigated his annoyance. Know about high sugar nourishments, however, as they can prompt emotional episodes, which aggravate you feel by tossing your body's insulin levels into mayhem.

Get sufficient rest. Keep normal rest times and have a mitigating routine before bed. Indeed, even have a go at improving your room or dispose of the bed you imparted to the narcissist if old recollections keep you conscious. Tune in to calm music, read, or diary. Try not to invest energy directly before bed doing whatever will raise considerations of outrage about the narcissist or fears about your future.

Invest energy in customary loosening up schedules for your body—get a back rub, invest time in a hot tub or sauna, take a hatha yoga class, set aside effort to extend your muscles a few times each day. Outrage, dread, and bitterness all will in general trigger muscles to tense. At the point when you are tense, your blood stream is undermined, and you'll experience difficulty thinking and will tire all the more effectively.

Exercise is one of the least expensive and best approaches to manage sadness, nervousness, and stress. Whenever your body is moving, extending, and dynamic, you'll feel progressively able, cheerful, certain, and less cynical. Discover a type of activity you especially like. Setting off to a class or having somebody to practice with can help propel you to keep at it. You need your body and psyche to work just as conceivable as you face these progressions and settle on choices about what to do next in your life. Shockingly, when you feel the most exceedingly awful, it very well may be simply the hardest time to treat with consideration and sympathy. You may believe you're too worn out to even think about exercising, yet take it gradually and move your body any way you can—even only a stroll around the square. As you feel better genuinely, you'll additionally feel better intellectually and inwardly. At the point when you take great consideration of your body, your cerebrum enrols that you are commendable, significant, and significant. This is a decent beginning to upgrading your confidence.

Self-Encouragement

The narcissist persistently invested energy mentioning to you what you didn't do right, and all things considered, those messages are as yet playing in your brain. It requires cognizant exertion and thoughtfulness regarding change these messages. You can't simply push them away. You need to effectively remove them with positive support and consolation. It generally feels great when others are the ones giving you that consolation, however somebody can't generally be close by. You're the main individual who is consistently there, so you're really amazing one to assume the job of encourager.

At the point when you're apprehensive, debilitated, and feeling alone, it very well may be hard to confront the entirety of the progressions and misfortunes you're encountering. The following stage is to make sense of what emotions you might want to have rather and afterward build up the solidarity to acknowledge them. That quality is cultivated fundamentally by your own self-consolation and promotion. What you state to yourself is crucially significant. You might not have been giving a lot of consideration to your own internal monolog, so begin seeing now how you converse with yourself.

Give Yourself Time

Recuperating a harmed confidence requires some serious energy and exertion. The more you were in the association with the narcissist, the more it might take. Passionate and mental change is certifiably not a convenient solution. Much the same as building muscle quality, it takes practice to change these old propensities and inner messages. Consider building your internal identity encourager a similar way you see heading off to the rec centre to fabricate your body. Get into a daily practice. With predictable exertion and consideration, the outcomes will be certainly justified regardless of the exertion.

CHAPTER 4: BUILDING RESILENCE

Flexibility is your capacity to bob again from destructive, injurious, or frustrating occasions. You are expanding your flexibility through the mending that you are doing now. Your degree of sense of pride, self-esteem, moral standards, and capacity to successfully support yourself all add to enthusiastic flexibility.

Sense of pride

You Are Worthy

Feeling commendable doesn't imply that you're superior to any other individual. It implies that you esteem yourself as beneficial to think about, care for, and secure. It additionally implies that you pay attention to yourself and your needs and you give them worth and significance in your life. Without a feeling of self-esteem, you can't tune in adequately to your own qualities, force, and rights, nor would you be able to focus suitably to your own needs or secure yourself. Your propensity to consistently put the requirements of others before your own, without expecting and demanding that your needs be reacted to, lessened your own feeling of self-esteem and made you helpless against control and control. The requirements of others are significant, however so are yours. A sound parity is required for enthusiastic prosperity.

Individuals will normally regard you at the level you permit, energize, and anticipate. Notice how the individuals who sincerely love you act toward you. How can it feel? Utilize this to give you significant data about your feeling of self-esteem. Notice as well if your inward self-messages are certain and empowering, or in the event that they are belittling and insolent. In the event that you consider yourself insignificant, weak, inadequate, or a disappointment, you're making way for others to likewise think and act toward you as though these things are in reality evident.

Act naturally Responsive

How willing would you say you are to react to your own emotions, needs, and needs? At the point when you overlook your own passionate self-care, you're demonstrating an uninterested and ill-bred frame of mind toward your own prosperity. Caring reactions incorporate approaching others for help, taking great physical consideration of yourself, thinking about your enthusiastic needs, talking your contemplations and emotions, and being as thoughtful to your own decisions as you are to the decisions of others. As a grown-up, you're answerable to do these things for yourself. In the event that you don't show an enthusiasm for dealing with your needs, it passes on the message that somebody ought to do it for you, which ordinarily pulls in controlling and ruling individuals.

Support Yourself

Taking a stand in opposition to what you think, need, and decide to do is fundamental for proper sense of pride. On the off chance that you're not talking your fact, at that point you're not so much present and taking part completely in your life and on the planet. You don't need to be bossy about it. Simply offer your thoughts and inclinations when others are doing as such. Rather than continually conceding to other people, stand up and battle for what you need to do probably a portion of the time.

Others may remark on your difference in conduct. Try not to stress. Individuals who see you and like you will really be pleased to get notification from you. At the point when others comprehend what you think, feel, and need, they are in reality progressively agreeable around you since they recognize what's in store. They'll feel that you genuinely care and are to a greater degree a member in the relationship and less of an eyewitness. It really carries you closer to others as they find a good pace better.

Grasp Your Ethical Principles

Follow Your Moral Compass

Everybody who has been involved with a narcissist has lied, yielded, or concealed the narcissist's awful or hostile practices to prop the relationship up. Conflicting with your standards and what you feel is correct is disheartening to your confidence and channels your internal quality and individual force. On the off chance that you don't like what you're doing, you won't like yourself. At the point when you rationalize the narcissist, it destroys your confidence.

Presently is a decent time to reset your ethical compass and follow your actual way. On the off chance that something doesn't feel right, at that point it isn't what you should do. Try not to work yourself out of your own standards and moral models, and don't let any other person work you out of them either. The outcomes are rarely good.

Distinguishing the practices and circumstances that have conflicted with your norms right now help you re-enter your dignity. At that point you can be set up to choose what moves you need to make to shield yourself from surrendering to those things once more. At the point when you completely grasp your qualities and life standards, it's simpler to stand firm on what you need and decide to do. You increase internal quality and versatility when you act from your moral place to ensure yourself. Let your measures direct you to the activities and connections that are beneficial for you.

Be Your Own Judge

You feel more prominent individual quality when you assume control over the duty of deciding for yourself whether you are making the best choice. You reserve the privilege to choose what is beneficial for you, what you need to do, and with whom you need to be included. Utilize your standards, sentiments, interests, and objectives to manage you into the circumstances and connections that you find satisfying and fulfilling. At the point when you choose for yourself what is best for you, you become increasingly engaged.

Leave your soul alone your guide—not your blame. Partners time and again settle on their decisions dependent on how liable or apprehensive they feel. This can manoeuvre you into and keep you in circumstances and connections that are unmistakably not bravo. Putting together your decisions principally with respect to the necessities and wishes of others is foolish. Keep in mind, your main duty in life is to deal with your own enthusiastic and physical prosperity, and afterward offer consideration to other people—not the different way. It's a similar standard as on planes, where you're told to put without anyone else breathing apparatus before you help other people. It's a matter of endurance.

Be your own judge in figuring out what you see, feel, and think and what decisions you should make. This is your life; you find a good pace. All things considered, you need to manage the results of these choices, regardless of whether you yield to another person or you decide for yourself.

Associate with Others Who Share You're Values

It is a lot simpler to follow your qualities when you're around others with the equivalent core values. At that point when you feel uncertain about a choice, you have other people who realize you well and can assist you with figuring out your issue. And still, at the end of the day, recollect that an official conclusion is your obligation. Continuously make sure to be careful of individuals who attempt to persuade you that their answer or recommendation is the main right one or compel you to settle on a specific decision.

Tune in to Your Gut

You may fear, in light of current circumstances, that you'll be deceived again by the narcissist. Narcissists don't generally leave and remain away. On the off chance that things don't work out how they would have preferred in their new life, they may return and attempt to reconnect. Also, on the off chance that you have youngsters together, you'll need to continue associating with the narcissist for quite a while to come. By what means will you keep yourself sincerely solid, focused, and sound?

Tune in to your gut rather than your blame, dread, or pity. Your gut is the focal point of your instinct and originates from your senses, recognitions, and regular body responses. It's an unquestionably progressively precise technique for mentioning to you what you really feel and need than your cognizant mind. At the point when you were with the narcissist, you needed to shut your gut instinct down in light of the fact that it was time and again in strife with what you thought you needed to do or ought to do to satisfy him.

A decent strategy for keeping in contact with your instinct is to check out your body.

At the point when you have to know rapidly how you feel about something, focus on how your stomach and mid-region feel. Analysts consider this zone of the body the second brain. It can't be subverted by the "should" and "ought to have" that you've been educated to believe are fitting. It lets you know unmistakably what you truly need and feel. Notice any general body indications of strain or torment too. Is your neck firm? Is it true that you are getting a cerebral pain? Is your lower back harming? Feelings turn out in a split second in your body. When your body is loose and quiet, you'll feel more joyful, however when your gut is in trouble, something isn't directly with your reality.

Your gut is the centre of your fight, flight, and freeze reactions. In caretakers, the most common response to distress is to freeze. To deal more effectively with narcissists, you've got to marshal your inner strength, which can't be done if you're in freeze mode. When situations are demanding or challenging, do you shut down and can't think of what to say and can't seem to focus your brain? That's freeze mode. When you feel instantly enraged and your mind is moving at super speed, that's fight mode. Obviously, if you just want to get away from the situation, you're in flight mode. These are all indicators that you need to protect yourself and get to a safe place so you can calm down and bring your rational thinking back online. Until you do that, you'll feel afraid, weak, and confused.

Narcissists try to push you to make quick responses and decisions. They sense when you're shut down and defenceless and choose that time to pressure or threaten you to get what they want. When your strength is drained and you're scared, your ability to think is compromised. Getting out of these fear modes allows you to marshal your inner strength, get your thinking cleared, and not cave in to these tactics.

Give yourself time to tune in to your body messages, calm yourself, and identify what you're feeling and why you're reacting as you are. Then spend some time thinking clearly about what you want. This may take minutes, hours, or sometimes days. Give yourself whatever time you need for this process and don't cave into pressure from the narcissist to respond immediately.

Identify Your Rights

There are two important kinds of rights that you need to embrace to increase your sense of power—you're legal rights and your humanity rights. If you own property or have children or legal obligations with a narcissist, you need to make sure you know your legal rights in your state. The *moment* you figure out that your partner is a narcissist, you need to consult a lawyer because at some point, you'll have conflicts with the narcissist over whatever you share.[3] If you know your legal rights, then you know where you stand, what to fight for, and what to expect. Narcissists are extremely good at trying to drain your power and emotional strength by creating mythical rights, threatening to "take everything," and making demands that aren't necessarily lawful. Knowing your legal rights can go a long way to allaying your fears, empowering you, and preparing you for the decisions you need to make.

Your humanity rights are more about your sense of emotional safety, well-being, positive regard, respect, self-worth, strength, and trust. These are things for which you rightfully get to set the standards. If you haven't clearly established your standards for these rights, then now is a good time to do so. Don't assume that everybody has the same ones.

Your standards are based on your own sense of self-worth and self-respect. Definitely take time to spell out your expectations and preferences in friendships, with family, and in intimate relationships. These help you identify whether you're in a relationship that is good for your well-being and happiness.

Clarify Your Obligations

As an adult, you have the right to choose what you will and won't do for others, how often you want to do these things, and in what way. Just because the narcissist called you selfish and accused you of not doing enough for him doesn't mean that it was true. You'll feel stronger and more empowered when you decide for yourself what obligations you choose to take on and what you expect in return.

Obligations are reciprocal, for example, parent to child and child to parent, husband to wife and wife to husband, employer to employee and employee to employer, or friend to friend. Your self-worth increases when you hold others to the same standard of meeting obligations to which you hold yourself.

So when you fulfil your commitments and the other person doesn't, you've got the right to choose whether you'll continue the relationship, terminate your promises to the other person, or get help and support to enforce your rights.

Obligations freely chosen reduce the likelihood of resentment and bitterness and increase positive connections with others. Keep working to find enjoyable reciprocal relationships, and you'll find your feelings of integrity, self-worth, and strength increasing.

Make Your Own Choices

When you clearly and consciously make your own choices, you'll feel stronger, more competent and powerful, and happier. Conversely, giving up what you want in order to keep others from complaining and whining will cause you to feel insignificant and resentful. When you always just go along with what others choose, you can end up believing that you don't have choices. This dilutes your strength. Even when the options are not what you would like, make a choice. You'll feel better and more in control of your life. Kendra used a self-talk exercise to help her figure out what to do about her mother and father. Following is the process.

Giving yourself specific instructions can include reminders to keep calm, instructions about what to do and say, and even directions about what feelings to have. This is reassuring and encouraging and keeps your conscious brain engaged and in charge. As a result, your mind is more able to override your fight, flight, or freeze reactions. It helps you create a plan, decide what you are going to do, and encourage yourself to do it.

Affirm you are capable. Continue talking to yourself using your first name. State all of the strengths and abilities you have that can help you get through this difficult situation. Avoid saying fearful, negative, or disaster-vision self-comments. Be encouraging.

After you get through the challenging encounter, be sure to identify what was successful and the specific strengths and actions that were helpful to you. This will increase your ability to meet the next challenging situation.

Being resilient includes respecting yourself, seeing your own worth, knowing what you think and feel, identifying and following your own values, and believing that you have the right to evaluate your own. To do these things, you have to listen to your deep emotional responses and honour them when deciding what to do. You also need to identify your rights, stand up for them, and take over making your own choices. Learning a new, more empowering way to talk to yourself is key. Strength and trust in yourself grow when you listen to your feelings and needs, take charge of making your own choices, and let yourself be authentically you.

CHAPTER 5: FORGIVENESS

Absolution is a characteristic stage during the time spent mending. It starts when you surrender your hatred and requirement for vengeance or compensation. Pardoning normally verges on feeling like everything is ok and accommodated with what has occurred and you're prepared to let the past be as it was and push ahead. It assists with having a comprehension of what occurred and why so you can put what you've experienced in context. Lastly, when you've discovered importance in your agony and enduring, pardoning happens all the more effectively. Clearly, this requires some investment.

Driving yourself to pardon before you are prepared just causes you to feel contemptible, blameworthy, and deficient. Numerous years working with customers has made it understood to me that pardoning doesn't occur until you arrive at acknowledgment of the narcissist and yourself similarly as you seem to be. Over and over again individuals attempt to drive themselves to excuse before they are mended. Release yourself through the whole procedure of sorrow and mending. After you have seen the full extent of your association with the narcissist, you'll have a superior thought of what you are pardoning the narcissist for and furthermore have the option to excuse yourself for being exploited. They go together.

Compassion

Compassion versus Sympathy

Compassion is a noteworthy component during the time spent pardoning. In any case, compassion is effectively mistaken for compassion, and compassion isn't a successful method to arrive at absolution. Compassion is the profound comprehension of and empathy for someone else's sentiments, responses, and encounters, while compassion is really encountering the other individual's emotions and viewpoint. Guardians are truly adept at identifying, however evident sympathy can be increasingly subtle. In compassion, you are joining and going into the enthusiastic experience of the other individual. At the point when the narcissist was dismal, you felt hopeless as well; when he was furious, it set off your resentment; when he felt forlorn, you felt dependable. Compassion manoeuvres you into the experience, and thus, you become some portion of the show. It can in the long run trigger disdain in you in light of the fact that the other individual isn't thankful enough of your endeavours. Genuine sympathy doesn't enact disdain or a requirement for reimbursement.

Sympathy Requires Boundaries

Sympathy is really harder to do in light of the fact that it expects you to keep your limits. You stay one stage out of the dramatization. You are fixed on the other individual with profound sympathy while attempting to get their emotions. Remaining that one stage away permits you to be caring without being attracted to have an impact in the dramatization. This is actually what advisors train for quite a long time to do. It is additionally for what reason being sympathetic with individuals you profoundly love and are sincerely enmeshed with is amazingly troublesome. Narcissists expect and request thoughtful reactions from their friends and family. They need you to feel what they are feeling. They need their torment to be your agony. To pardon the narcissist, you'll must have the option to step out of the dramatization and see the involvement in some target point of view and comprehension. It is likewise difficult to arrive at pardoning when the narcissist's egotistical practices are as yet causing you torment.

Janice imagined that she was being sympathetic to Jason's clarifications about not having the option to send every last bit of her help instalments on schedule. His checks were coming later and later in the month until one month she didn't get a check. In the wake of chatting with her specialist, she understood that she really felt frustrated about him and not compassion. She had not been giving enough consideration to her own needs. She informed the head prosecutor and had the instalments made through the court. Later she discovered he didn't send the last check since he had utilized the cash for his special first night in Hawaii. Her compassion had permitted her to be harmed once more.

Sympathy Is Non-judgmental

Sympathy additionally expects you to be non-judgmental. There is no analysis in evident empathy. As you deal with pardoning the narcissist and yourself, you should know about any damages and offenses that you're despite everything clinging to and let them go. Giving up isn't equivalent to overlooking. It implies you never again replay the pernicious encounters over in your brain to get that shock of exemplary indignation or, then again, to fuel your thoughtful reconnection with the narcissist. Censuring yourself or the narcissist benefits neither of you in any way in the present. It won't delete what occurred, nor will it protect you later on.

At the point when you see and acknowledge the enthusiastic incapacity that is at the core of narcissism, it can make it simpler to be less critical. You don't need to relinquish your genuine perceptions, negative assessments, or even your aversion of the narcissist's practices. Pardoning is to a greater extent a nonpartisan position wherein you never again sincerely care about the narcissist comparable to yourself. You can see him from a separation, rather like the more odd he is.

Acknowledgment and Empathy

So how would you acknowledge the narcissist? At this point, you may have perused a few books or looked the Internet for data on understanding the narcissist. This book is intended to assist you with understanding your encounters with the narcissist. Your association with the narcissist is or was a confounded move dependent on hallucination and perplexity. To acknowledge the narcissist, it assists with understanding that you and the narcissist are very unique by the way you see the world, connections, love, duty, mindful, and significantly more. What's more, your two perspectives will never meet up. The narcissist isn't probably going to get you, nor is he liable to change.

Being compassionate methods seeing and holding in your mind these distinctions while simultaneously recognizing your regular humankind, questionability, and the mental unsettling influence that is or was a piece of your relationship. You can change what you do and turn out to be all the more genuinely solid, however the narcissist will most likely consistently be disabled and hindered in his capacity to do as such. Recognizing the narcissist's harmed rationale, low sympathy, and flawed knowledge can assist you with moving to a progressively sympathetic position without losing your own perspective.

Trying to Understand

Usually it's much easier to forgive accidental behaviours than intentional ones. However, it's very difficult, even for professionals, to sort out which of the narcissist's behaviours are due to their poorly functioning brain wiring, what they have learned they can get away with, or what they do on purpose just to get their own way. You have no ability to make the narcissist change, and he has little chance of significant self-understanding. So this confusion will probably remain.

Mental Illness

Narcissism is considered to be an "enduring and pervasive" mental illness. Without insight, enormous determination, and constant self-surveillance of their behaviour's, narcissists cannot make the changes that would be necessary for them to give you what you would rightfully expect in a reciprocal relationship.

When you've been directly and negatively affected by these narcissistic responses, it may be difficult to have compassion for the narcissist's frantic, frightened, and delusional world. It's easier to reach forgiveness when you can separate your life from the narcissist's. When you have more distance and can keep your emotional boundaries, you can see and feel compassion for the narcissist's emotional illness more easily.

It Feels So Personal

Keep reminding yourself that nothing the narcissist says, does, feels, or thinks has anything to do with who you are or what you've done. Your best emotional protection is never to take anything—negative or positive—that the narcissist says or does as the real truth about yourself. Instead, rely on your own observations and the responses and feedback from friends and family who are emotionally healthy. When you disengage your self-esteem from the effect of the narcissist, you'll find yourself on more solid and sane footing. Knowing that narcissists are a whirling dervish in their own made-up world can help you move toward forgiveness.

Accept Human Frailty

No One Is Perfect

Coming to a sense of forgiveness is easier when you remember that no one is perfect. The narcissist has treated you badly, but you also know that you have not been your best self around him either. As you get to a point of restored wholeness and healing, it'll be easier to forgive such huge shortcomings and defects in the narcissist, as well as your own defensive reactions.

If you aren't ready to forgive yet, don't scold or judge yourself or demand that you get there right now. Be accepting of where you are. Acceptance of yourself "as you are" is a great foundation for eventual forgiveness. Remember that acceptance does not mean you agree with or condone these behaviour's. Rather it is a state of no longer protesting, demanding, or expecting the narcissist to be anything other than who he is.

What Part Did/Do You Play?

Because caretakers are usually too eager to accept responsibility for "making" the narcissist behave negatively, understanding your part in the drama is tricky. The narcissist behaves the way he does because of his own thoughts, feelings, and choices. So do you. Yes, it's easy to get pulled into demented and dysfunctional interactions with the narcissist, but you have a much greater ability to act differently than the narcissist does. You have greater control over your behaviour, and you don't have the narcissist's delusions.

When you no longer feel susceptible to the narcissist's manipulation, insults, and biased opinions, you're on the path to forgiveness. You may be surprised that taking responsibility for your own reactions around the narcissist can give your insight, confidence, and the courage to protect yourself better and be more forgiving. As you feel stronger and more in control of your life, you'll find that you are more compassionate and able to forgive the frailties of others.

Juanita hated the fights she used to get into with Manny. He would call her names or demean her suggestions, and she would instantly be angry and shout at him. It wasn't until after they were divorced that she understood how insecure and intimidated she had felt around him. When Juanita heard stories about his volatile moods from her two adult daughters, her anger would flare up again. However, the girls didn't get upset with their dad the way Juanita did. They'd just stay away from him when he was aggravating and then enjoy being with him when he was more positive. Eventually, Juanita saw that she'd been using anger to protect herself from pain and vulnerability. When she became more disengaged and cared less about Manny's opinions of her, she no longer needed anger to protect herself. It dwindled away, and so too did her old pain.

Practicing Humility

Not only did the narcissist grow up with other narcissists, but you too most likely grew up in a family with a parent or grandparent who had a personality disorder or similar behaviour's. You probably learned during childhood to accommodate, adapt, and resign yourself to crazy relationship patterns. However, a big difference is that you didn't inherit the brain wiring and emotional dysfunction that keeps the narcissist so mired in his contrary and skewed thinking and reacting. If you have a family member with a personality disorder, you were just plain lucky not to have inherited the same disability. You can see the misery he has in his life and the misery he causes for others. You've had many challenges caused by the narcissist in your life; however, I doubt that you'd ever choose to exchange places with him. You can get away from the effects of those inner demons, but the narcissist can't.

Let Go of Grievances

Let Go of Trying to Control and Punish

Forgiveness includes letting go of trying to control or punish the narcissist for his behaviors. You definitely need to protect yourself from future harm as much as possible. However, trying to change narcissists, giving them ultimatums, or stipulating behaviors that must be accomplished before you forgive only keeps you entangled in continuing turmoil and dysfunction. It isn't your job, nor is it possible, for you to make the narcissist see his mistakes or change his behaviors. Forgiveness isn't dependent on the other person's shaping up or changing. You are not the monitor of the narcissist's behaviour. Forgiveness is about your letting go.

Discharge Your Shame and Guilt

You'll keep on being up to speed in disgrace and blame on the off chance that you keep on believing you're liable for the narcissist's states of mind and practices. At the point when you completely understand that the narcissist's feelings and viewpoint are never again critical to you, your disgrace and blame will relax and break up. Pardoning originates from a position of acknowledgment of yourself and the other individual. There is no space for disfavour, mortification, or culpability. Continue keeping an eye on how your disgrace and blame are recuperating and dissolving, and notice how you feel more grounded as you let them go.

Relinquish Resentment and Revenge

Disdain and retribution emotions eat at your prosperity and do nothing to transform anything about the narcissist. Any solid, negative emotions you have toward the narcissist will be utilized by him to keep you joined and enmeshed. When you become the narcissist's foe, he will appreciate seeing you irritated and furious. Narcissists feed off any vitality, both negative and positive, that you send toward them. You may think you'd get a sentiment of fulfilment from seeing the narcissist squashed, however that is generally fleeting and doesn't have any kind of effect in your future. Proceeding onward with your own life toward adoration, delight, and happiness is your best retribution.

Find New Meaning

Finding new significance and reason in your life as the aftereffect of what you've endured can help a lot toward moving you toward pardoning. Expounding on this issue and offering assistance to other people who have been hurt by it have driven me to a more profound comprehension of my own encounters and expanded my quality and flexibility immensely. Robert Enright, conspicuous scientist and creator on absolution, says,

there are numerous approaches to discover importance in our enduring . . . concentrate more on the magnificence of the world or choose to offer help to others in need . . . talking your fact . . . reinforcing your inward purpose . . . [and] utilize your enduring to turn out to be all the more adoring and to pass that adoration onto others. Discovering importance, all by itself, is useful for discovering course in forgiveness.

What experiences, new abilities, and more prominent getting, quality, and empathy have you picked up right now mending? In the event that you experience difficulty seeing those for yourself, ask your loved ones to assist you with making a rundown. Approving what you've picked up helps you're recuperating more than seeing what you've lost. At the point when you consider yourself to be harder, firmer, and more grounded, you'll see that pardoning is progressively regular.

You're presently getting familiar with yourself than you may have ever needed to learn. What are you going to do with this new data? How might you utilize these new bits of knowledge to make your life and the lives of others better? What openings have opened up? What new headings for your energies and capacities would you say you are finding? How might you utilize these provoking encounters to effectively utilize what you have realized?

Finding a good pace

The pardoning of others, and particularly the narcissist, is significant for your total recuperating. You may get yourself ready to pardon certain words or activities however not others. Take it each piece in turn. Excuse what you can, and continue chipping away at giving up. A few things can take a long time to completely discharge. For instance, one customer couldn't excuse her previous spouse for prodding and disparaging her kids until they arrived at adulthood. Simply after she had proof that they were solid, competent, and not permanently hurt might she be able to at long last let go of her indignation and arrive at absolution.

Absolution Changes You, Not the Other Person

Absolution may support the other individual, yet basically it rolls out significant improvements in you. It is the last advance in your mending. At the point when you pardon someone else, something within you relinquishes the last bit of exploitation. It most likely won't totally dispose of your damage or even the entirety of your resentment, despite the fact that it may. It's a demonstration that originates from quality and furthermore invigorates you. It encourages relinquishing your ruminating, threatening vibe, and fierceness. Persistently contemplating past damage will keep that memory in the present, while absolution releases it. Absolution carries you to harmony and permits the terrible occasion to retreat into your memory, where it ought to be.

You don't have to tell the narcissist that you excuse him. Truth be told, I don't suggest it. An irate narcissist will utilize it against you eventually, and a narcissist who has proceeded onward couldn't care less. Narcissists don't think they have done whatever warrants pardoning in any case, so what's the point? Narcissists will in general be incensed or contemptuous of your endeavours, and that reaction can be recently harming.

Pardoning Yourself

Pardoning is a two-section process. You pardon others when they have hurt or defrauded you, however being exploited right now and independent culture quite often brings sentiments of blame and disgrace. You might resent yourself for being artless, taken in, or abused. Without a doubt, you additionally had your own guarded, irate responses to the narcissist's practices that you feel regretful about.

It might assist you with knowing that even prepared proficient specialists are routinely controlled by narcissists and react improperly. Narcissists are sharp and exceptionally energetic to separate your enthusiastic protections. They are magnificent on-screen characters and incredibly skilled at ensuring themselves. They completely accept that every other person is answerable for how they feel and what they do, so no contending or rationale will influence their suppositions. You wind up feeling angered and silly.

What number of others do you realize who have been hoodwinked and misdirected by the narcissist in your life? Do you think those individuals are dumb, stupid, or foolish? Do you judge them for falling under the thrall of the narcissist's appeal? On the off chance that you wind up censuring or making a decision about them adversely, at that point you are likely despite everything feeling deceived and should keep on chipping away at pardoning yourself. Continue dealing with seeing your qualities and esteeming your benefits while relinquishing your disgrace and blame. This procedure can take additional time than you may anticipate.

Proceeding onward

It's Not About Forgetting

I don't think the familiar maxim "Forgive and never look back" is an astute decision for partners. Narcissists like to bypass their mischievous activities, deny the hurt they have caused, and bait you into feeling blame or disgrace for your responses. You would prefer not to get quieted into intuition the narcissist will be more pleasant later on. For whatever length of time that the narcissist is a major part of your life in any capacity, be set up to redirect, separate, and shield yourself from potential mischief. One reason you remained for such a long time right now was your psychological arrangement to lessen and overlook the narcissist's damaging practices. It will keep on being significant that you know the narcissist will continue carrying on similarly as he generally has. Try not to expect anything diverse until, and on the off chance that, you ever observe long haul changes in his temperaments and practices. Absolution doesn't imply that you overlook the truth of the narcissist's pompous and destructive practices. Continuously be readied.

Outrage Doesn't Protect You

You may think you need to clutch your indignation to shield yourself from ever being deceived or controlled again. Outrage doesn't secure you. You were likely every now and again irate all through your association with the narcissist, yet that outrage didn't shield you from getting injured, nor did it stop the narcissist's practices.

Outrage is a solid fiery feeling. It can get you spurred and initiated to deal with yourself; leave the relationship; or to take on new and unnerving undertakings, for example, finding a new line of work, moving out, and being without anyone else. Be that as it may, when you're angry at the narcissist, you're despite everything appended, associated, and ensnared with him. Proceeded with outrage shows that you're still sincerely engaged with the narcissist. Withdrawal from the narcissist's capacity and impact over your feelings and your life is simply the best way to viably secure. Pardoning won't completely occur until your outrage has scattered enough that you never again get emphatically reactivated by the narcissist's new, offensive practices.

After you've pardoned practices of the past, it is your obligation to get yourself far from further harming collaborations. Your new quality, versatility, mindfulness, and comprehension of the narcissist and yourself will be preferable guards and insurance over annoyance.

Moving from Victim to Empowerment

The astounding thing about absolution is that it moves you from feeling like an unfortunate casualty to being engaged. It's a place of solidarity and power. It feels far superior to disgrace, blame, hatred, or dread. Recognizing what you've taken in and picked up from this difficult and challenging experience can free and empower you to push ahead. Pardoning encourages you consign your displeasure and hurt to the past. It's finished. Regardless of whether or when you have contact with the narcissist once more, you're always showed signs of change and a stronger individual. Your interest in his dramatization is finished.

Detach Your Energy from the Narcissist

Sincerely detaching and leaving is the best way to "win" and the best way to end the narcissist's control over you. It is your best insurance from further mischief and causes you recapture control over your own life. It's difficult to arrive at pardoning with somebody who is as yet doing likewise destructive practices toward you, however when you quit mindful and sincerely separate, you will feel more secure, more grounded, and additionally ready to excuse and proceed onward.

CHAPTER 6: FINDING OTHERS TO LOVE

Narcissist partners accept that in the event that they give enough love, they will be cherished in kind. This doesn't work with narcissists, who have a low capacity to adore others. Louise Hay, creator of You Can Heal Your Life, recommends that you top yourself off with affection, and afterward as you flood, send that extra out to other people.

This is love that won't exhaust you, won't leave you vacant and penniless, and won't relinquish you. In the event that somebody doesn't value your endowment of affection, you simply pull back, realizing that it won't leave you needing in light of the fact that you are continually topping yourself off. Moreover, this technique lessens fears of being distant from everyone else, disliked, or dismissed. How would you do this? There are three different ways to top off with affection—be available to adore from others, feel love from all inclusive vitality, and love yourself through self-care and a positive, empathetic mentality toward yourself.

Love from Others

Being around cherishing, strong individuals who are keen on your prosperity is imperative to your fondling filled. An excessive amount of detachment, a lot of time contemplating the past or the future, and over giving can prompt inclination vacant and desolate. You have to get consideration and approval from others—to be seen, heard, and reacted to. Others manoeuvre you into the present when you connect, which causes you to feel alive and blissful. You trade vitality with others and feel restored. Tolerating and permitting others to cherish you can do a great deal to top you off.

Creating Friendships

At the point when you leave an adoration relationship, it is enticing to need to discover a substitution as quickly as time permits. Be that as it may, as should be obvious, the way toward mending requires some investment, reflection, new mindfulness, and remaking. Putting resources into the great fellowships that you have and growing new ones are at the centre of this progression in your mending. Associations with companions can assist you with rehearsing progressively equivalent give-and-take. You can open up and share further pieces of yourself. You can evaluate new aptitudes, for example, defining limits, supporting yourself, and being progressively self-assured. With companions you can see yourself all the more equitably, practice abilities, and evaluate new reactions.

It's essential to have a strong arrangement of companions before returning into an affection relationship. You will require their help, just as their perceptions, understanding, and legitimate reactions to assess anybody new who comes into your life. You may not concur with all that they need to state, yet you can utilize this data to settle on better choices as you push ahead.

Opening to Love Again

Your previous partner job may have left you so depleted and wore out that you think you'll never need to be seeing someone. You may not believe your own capacity to see who will and won't be appropriate for you. Then again, you might be frantic to get into a relationship again to mitigate your agony and depression. For whatever length of time that you are in both of these states, you're likely not recuperated enough to pick shrewdly.

In any case, there will come when you are prepared. At the point when you feel content with your life and it feels full and upbeat, you'll end up willing and ready to impart your life to someone else. As you recuperate your passionate agony, reconstruct your confidence, and figure out how to acknowledge minding from others, you'll discover the existence you are searching for—or it might discover you.

Dread, franticness, misery, and tension would all be able to impede your being available to adore once more. As you mend the agony from an earlier time, you'll be prepared to pick who to carry nearer and who to move away from. Your standards will be controlling you instead of destitution or dread. Realizing that you can deal with yourself, you'll never again be edgy to discover somebody to make your life OK. You can start to depend on your sentiments to lead you toward individuals, encounters, and decisions that will reverberate with what your identity is and what you really need for your life.

Warnings

As you investigate new love connections consistently remain mindful of your reactions. Never markdown any fondling that comes. Think about your sentiments, instinct, and sharp perceptions, and utilize these to get yourself and the other individual. When you notice any feeling of things not feeling very right, advance back, watch, and give full thought to what you are taking note.

Whenever you get yourself awkward with how someone else is acting around you, promptly pay heed. Watch the conduct, notice your sentiments, and evaluate whether the communication is aware, adoring, mindful, and obliging of you. On the off chance that it isn't, step away from the communication, and give yourself an opportunity to reflect. It might likewise be shrewd to converse with somebody you trust about the circumstance to get point of view and input. At that point choose what you need to do or say. Take each new relationship gradually to give yourself an opportunity to confide in your new aptitudes and impulses.

What Are You Looking For?

What are you searching for? Have you at any point plunked down and worked out the characteristics you want in an accomplice or set up norms for the kinds of connections you long for? Have you made an image in your brain of how you two would cooperate, invest energy with one another and separated, resolve contrasts, coexist with one another's family, go through and set aside cash, split errands, and experience your sexuality?

Discussion about It Sooner Rather than Later

Try not to hold up until you conclude this is a genuine relationship to share your thoughts and sentiments about these things. Instructing yourself to keep a watch out what the other individual's thoughts are is a superintending reaction. The awesome preferred position of being open and clear about what your identity is, the thing that you feel, and what you incline toward from the minute you meet somebody is that you zero in more rapidly on whether the relationship will be good for you. It implies that you can sift through what won't work at an early stage before you get excessively genuinely dedicated. At that point you're more averse to go through months or years attempting to persuade each other to see things your way since you don't generally function admirably together. At the point when you utilize the cautious model, you'll as of now be genuinely and explicitly included before you even see whether the relationship can possibly work for you.

Try not to Overlook Good Possibilities

At the point when you were being a partner, your inclination was to search for an accomplice who truly required your assistance or somebody who might deal with you. Your enthusiastic radar was all the more unequivocally tuned to the individuals who were battling and requiring help or the individuals who appeared to be incredible, persuasive, and in charge. You may have totally disregarded and overlooked the potential accomplices in the middle.

What Love Really Feels Like

The genuine centre of adoration is acknowledgment. Feeling acknowledged similarly as you are gives you a gigantic feeling of harmony, trust, solace, and fearlessness. You know then that you don't have to fear dismissal, reprimand, or judgment. Contradictions are just about alternate points of view and don't include prevalence/inadequacy, great/terrible, affront, incitement, or injuring. Acknowledgment implies that mix-ups are essentially a trouble to be beaten together. In any event, when you dissent, you despite everything realize you are protected and adored.

Harmony

The most well-known inclination individuals have after this activity is a feeling of harmony and happiness. Smoothness, harmony, and amicability win where there is certified love. Once more, this doesn't preclude contrasts of sentiment, however these are acknowledged and worked out with thinking about the requirements and pride of the two individuals. No two people see, feel, and think precisely indistinguishable. A quiet relationship doesn't rely upon your being similar; rather it's tied in with acknowledging, esteeming, and in any event, respecting those distinctions, as they add to the entire prosperity of the relationship. I love the expression "the Loyal Opposition" as it's utilized in England. It essentially implies that restricting points of view can meet up to make more excellent arrangements, while staying faithful profoundly principles of the relationship. Being tranquil originates from the frame of mind of mindful, a longing for concordance, and regard for one another.

Aware

Regard incorporates regard, adoration, high respect, thankfulness, and affirmation. It doesn't require understanding, yielding, or quitting any pretence of anything. It implies taking the emotions and estimations of someone else truly. Did you feel regarded by the narcissist in your previous relationship? When and with whom have you felt regarded? Something contrary to regard is dismiss. At the point when you feel ignored or abhorred, you are not in a caring communication. At the point when others show regard for you, they aren't really concurring with you, however they are as yet respecting your worth, treating you compassionate, and paying attention to your needs and sentiments.

Empowering

Love is empowering. It moves you to be your best. You feel consoled. Your spirits are raised up, and you feel the vitality and boldness to push ahead. You positively don't feel miserable and vulnerable, as you did with the narcissist. You feel genuinely bolstered, sustained, and invigorated. Recollect when somebody gave you support. It might have been a parent, an educator, or a companion. What did that individual state and do that felt empowering? Make a note of the inclination. That is the thing that you are searching for in a long haul love relationship.

Opportunity

Love is about opportunity to act naturally. That doesn't mean opportunity to do anything you like—however opportunity to be what your identity is, with full certainty that the other individual thinks about you simply the manner in which you are. You're allowed to have your own contemplations, emotions, qualities, dreams, and objectives, and you realize you'll despite everything be acknowledged, regarded, and energized by your cherished one. The dread of being opposed or deserted melts away. You realize you are cherished for yourself, not only for what you accomplish for the other individual.

Equality

In a loving relationship, neither person dictates, controls, or demands that his or her ideas and rules will rule. It's a joint effort to create a life together that is comfortable and supportive for both of you. You may each contribute different things to the relationship, but both receive equal consideration. As a result, power struggles and resentment become negligible. Neither person tries to control or dominate the other.

CHAPTER 7: KNOWING YOUR INTENTION (CONCLUSION PART)

As you've read this book, I'm certain you've been considering your own circumstance and attempting to relate every thought displayed here to what you've been encountering. I trust you've discovered the thoughts supportive and material. You may have even understood that the recuperation from your association with this narcissist is actually what you have expected to turn into the individual you need to be. The way to recovering yourself takes vitality, boldness, and assurance. You've most likely become familiar with narcissism than you at any point needed to know, and ideally you won't have to utilize that agonizing training particularly later on. Nonetheless, what you've found out about yourself is precious in light of the fact that you'll take that information with you. It's the premise of making the existence you need to have now. As you make sense of what's essential to you bit by bit, you'll have numerous new chances to utilize those revelations.

You're never again a fell, sad, frightful guardian. You realize that your considerations, emotions, and necessities are significant enough for you to invest your time and vitality making sense of them and affectionately reacting to them. Presently the time has come to set your expectation for how you need to push ahead.

An expectation is fundamentally an assurance to act with a particular goal in mind. It's a determination—an approach to centre your energies—in view of your standards and objectives. It's anything but a goals in the basic utilization of the word. Time after time goals are made on account of what you figure you ought to do. This is tied in with choosing to respect, backing, and regard completely what your identity is by staying alert and present in your life. It's not tied in with doing anything effectively or impeccably or doing it to it would be ideal if you fix, or help any other individual. It's tied in with choosing to be alive for yourself. It's tied in with getting things done in a way that is completely harmonious with what your identity is.

Discharge Yourself from the Expectations of Others

As a guardian you urgently needed and sat tight for authorization, acknowledgment, and comprehension from the narcissist. Presently you see that you could never have gotten those things from the narcissist, regardless of what you did. In a tangled manner, this really discharges you from until kingdom come stressing over winning the narcissist's endorsement. It's a difficulty, with the goal that releases you from squandering your vitality on it any more.

Be that as it may, being the decent individual you are, you'll likely additionally need to chip away at relinquishing attempting to if it's not too much trouble fix, and help a portion of the others in your life. Keep in mind, what you accomplish for others has worth and you have to pick cautiously where you burn through that effort. You can deal with yourself and provide for other people, when you remember the standard of correspondence. Getting things done for other people or to satisfy others makes reliance and threatening vibe. Be a guide to others by keeping up your limits, while as yet being open and responsive.

Making Your Intention

Investigate your core values and the facts you have found out about yourself through the previous parts of this book. See whether you can place into one sentence the general feeling of these exercises. Here are a few models:

- I've chosen to have a quiet, genuinely safe home with cherishing, delicate individuals around me.
- I'm a mindful, liberal individual, and I hope to be around others such as myself.
- I carry on with a real existence dependent on my decisions, not the decisions others make for or about me.
- Whatever I provide for other people, I likewise provide for myself.

These are expectations. They express a centre conviction, an objective, and a purpose to get it going. They help you set the measures of what you expect and are eager to endure; keep your limits; and maintain a dream of yourself, which at that point turns into the reason for your everyday choices.

Make a move

Goals lead to activities. Much more altogether, goals clarify what your activities will be, with next to no exertion at the time. In the event that you need a "quiet and sincerely safe home" you won't decide to associate with any individual who shouts, starts quarrel, affronts, or belittles you or does practices that alarm you. On account of your aim explanation, you'll know in a split second what you need to do in another circumstance since it will either satisfy your guidelines or it won't. In the event that it fulfils your guidelines, you advance toward the cooperation. In the event that it doesn't, you stop, delay, and choose the amount to move away. You don't need to invest any energy making sense of whether the other individual will like your choice, nor do you need to make sense of what the other individual needs or will say or do. You simply need to choose what you need to do about the cooperation. Do you perceive how this spares a huge measure of time, vitality, mental handling, and passionate anxiety? This is a lot easier than what you used to do.

It may not be anything but difficult to surrender your old guardian designs. Despite the fact that you comprehend picking your own behaviour, you may in any case be confounded when you get trapped in a troublesome or extraordinary circumstance with the narcissist. You'll realize that you're despite everything centred around the narcissist on the off chance that you are asking yourself such inquiries as "How would I get him to quit hollering?" "How would I escape this relationship?" "How would I get him to change how he acts toward me?"

Underlying these inquiries is a proceeded with trust that you can make a move and have the narcissist be more pleasant or give you authorization to act or that you can satisfy him about what you're doing. This is old guardian thinking, and you'll be befuddled about what to do. As a general rule you should simply choose what you need and afterward make suitable move. It's never again about making the narcissist think, feel, or favour of anything.

Your activities for your own prosperity shouldn't depend on the narcissist's doing anything any other way. Your activities can be as straightforward as hanging up the telephone, leaving, saying actually no, not answering to messages or instant messages, or not welcoming such an antagonistic individual to your home. By adhering to your aims, you basically don't take an interest in whatever doesn't meet your qualities and goals. At that point you're ready to grasp everything else with vitality and happiness.

Trust the Process

Being a guardian was tied in with attempting to be in charge of the circumstance, so it might be difficult for you to believe that things will turn out, particularly in light of the fact that they positively didn't work out how you would have preferred with the narcissist. Rather than controlling your own life's heading, you were attempting to control the narcissist's, which is truly like attempting to control the circle of Jupiter. At the point when you turn your concentration to settling on choices about your own life, you'll discover things turn out more effectively so then it's simpler to confide in the circumstance and yourself.

All through this book I've been sketching out a procedure that has demonstrated to be successful in helping partners completely change themselves to improve things. Similarly as with most new things, it might feel cumbersome, and you may battle with it from the outset. In any case, as you set up these recommendations as a regular occurrence, you'll feel more grounded and progressively certain and furthermore start to have more pleasant individuals around you. I firmly accept that you can make a superior life for yourself than you've had. I profoundly trust that you trust in yourself and have the mental fortitude to step forward.

Include the Good in Your Life

The speediest method to move out of feeling defrauded and miserable is to include the positive qualities throughout your life. Appreciation has an astonishing capacity to advise you that the challenges and agony in your life are extremely just a little piece of what's going on. By far most of the individuals throughout your life and the encounters you've had with them are basically positive. At the point when you invest an excessive amount of energy paying special mind to threat and catastrophe, you can overlook what is really functioning admirably.